Stormwarning

Kristín Svava Tómasdóttir

Translated from the Icelandic by K.B. Thors

**PHONEME
MEDIA**

Phoneme Media
P.O. Box 411272
Los Angeles, CA 90041

"Annað bréfið til herra Brown" and "Góðir tímar"
first appeared in *Skrælingjasýningin*
"Góðir tímar - útgáfa til upplesturs á leikskólum" first appeared in *Stína* 6:3
"Fallegar rústir" was written for *Höfuðverk*

ISBN: 978-1-944700-68-3
LOC: 2018936883

This book is distributed by Publishers Group West

Cover design and typesetting by Jaya Nicely

Printed in the United States of America

Phoneme Media is a nonprofit media company dedicated to
promoting cross-cultural understanding, connecting people and
ideas through translated books and films.

http://phonememedia.org

Stormwarning

EFNISYFIRLIT

TABLE OF CONTENTS

BÖBBLÍ Í VÚLVUNNI

Og svo bætti þessi sami fréttamaður gráu ofan á svart með því að segja:
...margir hafa það fyrir sið að skála í böbblí...skála í böbblí!
Líklega átti stúlkutetrið við kampavín eða freyðivín.

Eiður Svanberg Guðnason
fyrrverandi sendiherra

Við drekkum böbblí í Vúlvunni
og setjum það á rekstrarreikninginn
sleppum okkur!
pöntum dómínós

ostagott
súkkulaðigott
kanilgott og nutellagott
ég geymi gott og böbblí í klósettkassanum

stelpur ég á mér leynda fantasíu:
að sleikja heila hnetusmjörskrukku af spenntum
upphandleggsvöðva íþróttaálfsins
og reka hann svo í gegn með tálgaðri gulrót

BUBBLY IN THE VULVA

And then this same reporter added insult to injury by saying:
...many have grown accustomed to toasting with 'bubbly'...toasting with bubbly!
Probably the poor girl meant champagne or sparkling wine.

Eiður Svanberg Guðnason
former ambassador
grammarian blogger
Icelandic language authority

We drink bubbly in the Vulva
and put it on the business account
we let loose!
we order dominos

we get some
cheese
get some
chocolate
get some cinnamon candy and nutella
I stash sugar and bubbly in the toilet tank

girls I have this secret fantasy:
to lick a whole jar of peanut butter from the tense
tricep of Sportacus
and run him through with a whittled carrot

stelpur fyrr eða síðar
verður þetta líferni okkur að aldurtila

sækjum um frest
hugsum um formæðurnar
böbblí og brauðterturnar

úps ég setti of mikið majónesi
tertan riðar til falls
og í hvaða reit fer risnan?

ekki þessi leiðindi
ekki þetta stress
það er búið að vökva plönturnar í dag
búið að vekja
búið að svæfa
sækjum um frest
allt byrjar ekki aftur fyrr en á morgun

konur eiga eitt prósent af auðæfum heimsins
þar af eigum við
böbblí og kanilgott

kvenlegur dekadens
er bestur og klístraðastur

fáum okkur meira böbblí
böbblí í Vúlvunni

girls sooner or later
this lifestyle will be the death of us

let's apply for a rebate
let's think of our foremothers
bubbly and bread tarts

oops I put too much mayonnaise
the tart wobbles, about to fall
and how do we write-off hospitality?

enough hassle
enough stress
the plants have been watered today
the kids were woken up
the kids were put to bed
let's apply for a rebate
everything doesn't start again until tomorrow

women own one percent of the world's wealth
we include in that
the bubbly and cinnamon

feminine decadence
is the best and stickiest

let's get some more bubbly
bubbly in the Vulva

elskum þetta drasl þetta djönk þetta plast
kófheita pólýesterkrókódílabúninginn
blikkandi jólaseríur og gerviblóm
elskum þennan efnisheim
þessar gömlu vídeóspólur
nammibarsnjálginn og blautt malbik
elskum þessa ofgnótt
elskum þessa siðmenningu og frumstæðar hvatir hennar
v(ið)erum ekki hreinlynd
vonum að heimurinn tortímist í neistaflugi frá millistykkinu

we love that stuff that junk that plastic
the stifling hot polyester crocodile costume
blinking christmas lights and fake flowers
we love that material world
these old videotapes
candy bar pinworms and wet asphalt
we're loving this excess
loving this civilization and her primitive impulses
our conscience is not c(lean)
we're hoping the world will be destroyed by flying sparks
    from the adapter

UPP VIÐ FOSSINN LUBBA

LUBBI
þar sem héraðsmótið náði hámarki
LUBBI
þar sem fyllibyttan datt í lækinn
LUBBI
þar sem lyngið ilmar
LUBBI
þar sem fjalldrapinn grær
LUBBI
þar sem eimingartækin krauma
LUBBI
krútt
LUBBI
náttúra
LUBBI
krúttúra
LUBBI
þar sem ég lifi ekki í sífelldum ótta við skordýr
LUBBI
best í heimi
LUBBI
ættbókin fylgir
(LØBBE
ekki lengur undir dönksum yfirráðum)

RETREAT TO THE LUBBI WATERFALL

RETREAT

where the county picnic reaches its height

RETREAT

where the drunk falls into the stream

RETREAT

where it smells of heather

RETREAT

where the dwarfbirch grows

RETREAT

where the distiller simmers

RETREAT

darling

RETREAT

nature

RETREAT

darlingnature

RETREAT

where I do not live in constant fear of insects

RETREAT

the best in the world

RETREAT

genetics included

(RE/TREAT

no longer under Danish control)

LUBBI
langt inni í landi
LUBBI
þegar siðmenningin hrynur
LUBBI
þegar rigningin súrnar
LUBBI
þegar vatnið vex
LUBBI
þegar enginn veit hvað gerist næst
LUBBI
þegar logar í Drekanum
og gjörningaveður geisar á Halanum
þér skrikar fótur í brattanum á flóttanum
og járnhöndin í hanskanum
og augu þín blindast af blossanum
og höfuð þitt bráðnar á koddanum
og glittir í hvítt í hnakkanum á djáknanum

RETREAT

far inland

RETREAT

when civilization crumbles

RETREAT

when the rain gets sour

RETREAT

when the water rises

RETREAT

when no one knows what will happen next

RETREAT

when the Dragon catches fire

and storms rage on the Tail

your feet slip on the slope as you flee

and the iron hand is in the glove

and your eyes go blind from the flash

and your head melts on the pillow

and the skull of the deacon gleams white

PASSÉ

Einu sinni vildu allir komast til tunglsins.
Það tókst sumarið 1969.
Síðan langar engan lengur til tunglsins.
Tunglið er autt og yfirgefið.

PASSÉ

Once everyone wanted to get to the moon.
It happened the summer of 1969.
Then no one longed for the moon.
The moon is empty and abandoned.

GRÓÐURHÚS

Geislavirkur birtukúpull
yfir snævi þakinni jörð

þrisvar á sólarhring er slökkt
svo plönturnar haldi að það sé komin nótt
leggst þá þunglyndi yfir mennska þegna
þessa varma lands

GREENHOUSE

Radioactive lightblock
on snow-covered ground

three times a day it is turned off
so the plants think night has come
and depression overwhelms the human subjects
of this thermal country

ANNAÐ BRÉFIÐ TIL HERRA BROWN

Fékkstu aldrei frá mér bréfið herra Brown?
það var himinbleikt og glimmerstráð og ég hellti yfir það
ilmvatni úr prufu
herra Brown „ég er bara stelpa
sem stendur fyrir framan strák
og biður hann að elska sig"
lít ég út fyrir að vera hryðjuverkamaður?

Ég er allt annar maður með víni
annar maður með víni ég er meiri maður sterkari og stærri
maður
með víni

græðgin, metorðagirndin, öfundsýkin brjálæðislega
eru ekki eiginleikar sem eru mér eiginlegir
hrokinn, lygin, undirferlið, sjálfselskan — nei!
þungu fargi hefur verið af mér létt

nú get ég loksins sýnt mitt rétta andlit
nú get ég loksins sýnt mitt blíða, friðsæla og nægjusama andlit
stundum eru augun í mér svo blá
að þau skelfa mig í speglinum
lít ég út fyrir að vera hryðjuverkamaður?

ANOTHER LETTER TO MR. BROWN

Did you never receive my letter Mr. Brown
it was sky blue and sparkly and I doused it
with perfume from a tester
Mr. Brown, "I am just a girl
standing in front of a boy
asking him to love her"
do I look like a terrorist?

I am a totally different person with wine
a different person with wine I am more of a person a stronger and bigger
person
with wine

greed and megalomania, envy and malice
are not are not really characteristic of me
pride, deceit, duplicity, selfishness—no!
a heavy weight has been lifted

now I can finally show my true colors
now I can finally show my tender, peaceful, cheerful colors
sometimes my eyes are so blue
they scare me in the mirror
do I look like a terrorist?

þú ert kallinn, herra Brown
ég er bara fórnarlamb þessara aðstæðna
þessara erfiðu aðstæðna
möppudýr í ríki illskunnar

ég hef mjög þroskaða sýn á hið borgaralega samfélag
og ég segi:
er enginn að hugsa um börnin?
villudýrin á mörkinni, þau grimmu leonin og hinar ólmu birnur
vanrækja ekki sitt fóstur
en þú, herra Brown, það er nú eitthvað annað
látum ekki börnin anda að sér tóbaksreyk
látum þau ekki anda að sér þrúgandi andrúmslofti
skrælingjasýningarinnar
líta þau út fyrir að vera hryðjuverkamenn?

ég hef mjög þroskaða sýn á þjóðarlíkamann
og ég er ansi hrædd um að oft þurfi að ampútera við öxl
látum ekki börnin anda að sér tóbaksreyk
vísum þeim ekki til sætis með misindismönnunum

herra Brown
ég hef sent þér bréf
ég hef sýnt fullan samstarfsvilja
þér hafið ítrekað brugðist
þér hafið sýnt mér lítillækkandi framkomu
þér fáið ekki fleiri tækifæri, herra Brown
ég kýs að líta á þetta sem persónulega móðgun

you are the man, Mr. Brown
I am a mere victim of these circumstances
these difficult circumstances
a public servant in an evil state

I have a very mature view of civil society
and I say:
is no one thinking of the children?
animals in the wild, fierce lions and raging bears
do not neglect their young
you, Mr. Brown
are something else
do not let the children inhale tobacco smoke
do not let them inhale this oppressive atmosphere
do they look like terrorists?

I have a very mature view of civil society
and I am afraid we must often amputate at the shoulder
do not let the children inhale tobacco smoke
do not let them sit beside sketchy characters

Mr. Brown
I have sent you a letter
I have shown complete willingness to cooperate
you have repeatedly failed
you have shown me diminishing returns
you do not get another chance, Mr. Brown
one could choose to regard this as a personal insult

á næsta bréfi verður ekkert glimmer. Ekkert glimmer, herra
Brown
ég lít ekki út fyrir að vera hryðjuverkamaður

the next letter will not sparkle. No glitter, Mr.

Brown

I do not look like a terrorist

ÞAÐ SEM EKKI MÁ

ég myndi aldrei fara á neinn af þessum plebbaskemmtistöðum
ég myndi aldrei bjóða börnunum upp á svona líf
ég myndi aldrei fara eftir því sem aðrir segðu mér bara til að
þóknast þeim
ég myndi aldrei leggja ólöglega í Svíþjóð
ég myndi aldrei henda plastflöskum í almennt rusl
ég myndi aldrei hlæja að barni sem læsti sig inni í skáp í
búningsklefanum
ég er bara ekki þannig týpa
ég myndi aldrei leggja út í það aftur að kaupa tékkneska flugvél
ég myndi aldrei kaupa spattaðan hest (nema á eitthvað smotterí)
ég myndi aldrei þora að púlla Pharcyde-tík
maður ætti líka að læra af reynslunni
ég myndi aldrei gera neitt til að meiða dýr eða þröngva þeim til neins
ég myndi aldrei drekka heila rauðvínsflösku einsömul á
þriðjudagskvöldi
ég myndi aldrei fá ættingja til að skrifa upp á
ég myndi aldrei grípa til ósannsögli
ég myndi aldrei senda vanhugsaðan tölvupóst
ég myndi aldrei tína skítuga sokka aftur upp úr óhreinatauskörfunni
sumt er einfaldlega ekki í boði

samt eru alls konar hlutir að gerast
sem ég vil ekki að komi fram í ævisögu minni

DO NOT

I would never go to any of these plebian entertainments
I would never impose a life like this upon children
I would never go by what others say just to please them
I would never park illegally in Sweden
I would never throw plastic bottles in the general garbage
I would never laugh at a child who locked themselves in the
    changing room locker
I am just not that type
I would never again venture to buy a Czechoslovakian plane
I would never buy a windsucking horse (except as some kind of joke)
I would never dare pull a bitch move
a person should learn from experience
I would never do anything to hurt animals or force them to do things
I would never drink an entire bottle of red wine alone on a
    Tuesday night
I would never get relatives to co-sign
I would never resort to lies
I would never send a thoughtless email
I would never wear filthy socks from the laundry basket
some things are simply not options

yet there are all kinds of things happening
I do not want to include in my biography

FLENSAN MÍN

þú veist að það er flensa að ganga
harmagráturinn bergmálar í eyrum þínum
en þú lætur þér standa á sama

annarra manna flensa
er áhrifalítil flensa

það er svo margt sem er að í heiminum
og í hinu stóra samhengi
og í þjóðfélagi nútímans
er fráleitt að veita inflúensu slíkt vald

svo kemur hún til þín

hún leggur undir sig líkama þinn
hún skríður fram útlimina
þú finnur hana í höfðinu
í húðinni
í andardrættinum
í þrýstingnum bak við augun
í sálinni sem skreppur saman og verður svo lítil og aum
að andleg reisn þín er eilíflega glötuð

og þú hugsar:
ó gjáin!
milli eigin flensu og annarra

MY FLU

You know there is a flu about
the keening echoes in your ears
but you make yourself go on the same

someone else's flu
is a flu of little consequence

there is so much to the world
and the greater context
and current society
it is absurd to grant influenza such clout

then she comes for you

she conquers your body
she creeps in through the limbs
you find her in your head
in skin
in breath
in the pressure behind the eyes
in the soul that shrinks and becomes so small and wretched
that your spiritual dignity is lost forever

and you think:
oh the gap!
between your own flu and another

Leita fróunar í örygginu
þar sem engin tækifæri eru framar

gömlum fasteignaauglýsingum:
það er eitthvað fólk löngu búið að kaupa þessi hús
komin ný og ljótari eldhúsinnrétting

búið að ráða í þessi störf

þetta veður löngu liðið

hinir dauðu ennþá dauðir

PASSÉ 2: PERIODICALS.IS.NET

searching for comfort or security
where the opportunities are no more

old real estate ads
people bought this house a long time ago
got new and uglier kitchen renovations

positions already filled

that weather long past

the dead are still dead

~

Ég skima eftir rottum á teinunum
þetta er hættulegur staður
hér eru þjófar og ræningjar
ég veit ekki af hverju nokkur
ætti að vilja meiða mig
ég sem er svo góð
en þetta er hættulegur staður
og það eru skuggalegir unglingar á vappi

~

I watch for rats on the tracks
this is a dangerous place
here there are thieves and robbers
I don't know why someone
should want to hurt me
I who am so good
but this is a dangerous place
and shady teens are hanging around

MARTRÖÐ UM FERMINGARVEISLU

Þú ert staddur í fermingarveislu.

Hún er haldin í daufgulum sal.

Salurinn er í eigu frímúrara.

Í salnum eru stórir gluggar.

Aprílsólin þrýstir á gluggana.

Hún er að bræða snjóinn sem þekur grasflötina fyrir utan.

Gluggarnir eru lokaðir.

Það er kæfandi hiti í salnum.

Í mollunni finnur þú lyktina af brauðtertum og gömlu fólki.

Fermingarbarnið er þér ókunnugt.

Þú þekkir engan í salnum nema foreldra þína.

Þú segir til nafns, í hvaða skóla þú ert og í hvaða skóla þú ætlar næst.

Þeim er alveg sama.

Þau eru strax búin að gleyma hvað þú heitir.

Þau gætu ekki haft minni áhuga á því hvaða mann þú hefur að geyma.

Þér er ómótt af marenstertunni.

Þú horfir út um gluggann.

Þig langar til að fara út og ganga í hringi kringum húsið þar til
þetta er búið.

Þig langar til að taka lúku af snjó og maka honum framan í þig og
troða honum inn á þig.

En þú sérð enga undankomuleið.

Það er búið að læsa dyrunum.

Það er búið að setja slagbrand fyrir.

NIGHTMARE ABOUT CONFIRMATION PARTY

You are standing at the confirmation party.
It is held in a dingy yellow hall.
The hall is owned by freemasons.
In the hall there are large windows.
The April sun presses on the windows.
It is melting the snow that covers the grass outside.
The windows are closed.
The heat in the hall is suffocating.
In the musty heat you can smell cakes and old people.
The confirmand is a stranger to you.
You know no one in the hall except your parents.
You say your name, which school you go to and which school you
    will go to next.
They don't care.
They have immediately forgotten your name.
They could not be less interested in the person you have in store.
You are sick with meringue.
You look out the window.
You long to go out and walk in circles around the place until this
    is done.
You long to take handfuls of snow and smear them on your face
    and stuff them into yourself.
But you see no escape.
The door has been locked.
The way has been barred.

Þú horfir á kaffibollana
og jakkafötin
og terturnar
og þú hugsar:
Ég kemst aldrei héðan út.

You look at the coffee cups
and the suits
and the tarts
And you think:
I will never get out of here.

GÓÐIR TÍMAR

Þetta voru góðir tímar. Ég starfaði slitrótt á blaðinu, eyddi kvöldunum hamrandi á ritvélina umvafin tóbaksreyk, en á daginn hitti ég stelpurnar. Við sátum á kaffihúsum löngum stundum, oftast á Sélect þar sem þjónarnir þekktu okkur, drukkum kaffi og apperitif. Einhver las línur úr nýjum ljóðabálki eða upp úr heimspekiritgerð, stundum flettum við blöðunum. Það var mikið talað, mikið hlegið, svo ráfuðum við um göturnar ölvaðar af eigin orðsnilld. Við vorum þarna ég og Simone, Svava, Gertrude, Emma, Rósa og fleiri, Victoria bættist í hópinn ef hún var góð af því viðsjárverða þunglyndi sem á það til að fylgja snilligáfunni. Við áttum ekki bót fyrir boruna á okkur en tókst alltaf að skrapa saman fyrir apperitif og nýjasta verki þess ljóðskálds sem við kusum að hæðast að þá stundina. Á endanum kvæntumst við flestar eins og gengur og hlýja heimilislífsins heillaði að vissu leyti — en við héldum auðvitað áfram að hittast meðfram, ævinlega á fimmtudagskvöldum, drukkum saman og fórum svo á hóruhús, þar sem við ræddum málin við skörpustu mellur Parísarborgar áður en við fórum með þeim í herbergið inn af.

GOOD TIMES

Those were good times. I worked intermittently on the paper, spending nights hammering on the typewriter in a cloud of tobacco smoke, but in the daytime I met up with the girls. We sat in cafes for long stretches, often at Sélect where the servers knew us, drinking coffee and aperitifs. Someone read lines from a new poem or philosophical essay, sometimes we'd flip through the news. There was a lot of talk, a lot of laughing, then we'd stroll through the streets drunk on our own words. We were there, Simone and I, Svava, Gertrude, Emma, Rósa and more, Victoria joined the group if she was well enough to risk the insidious depression that comes with genius. We didn't have enough for our tab but we always managed to scrape something together for the aperitifs and the latest work by the poet we chose to mock for the moment. In the end like most we got married and certainly enjoyed a warm homelife to some extent—but of course we kept on meeting up, every Thursday night, drinking together and then going to the whorehouse, where we discussed the issues with the sharpest hookers in Paris before going with them into their quarters.

JÁKVÆÐNI

Áfram fjöll!
Áfram ský!
Áfram mosi!

BEING POSITIVE

Go mountains!
Go clouds!
Go moss!

PASSÉ 3: RÓMANTÍSKT LJÓÐ
UM KAPÍTALISTA FORTÍÐARINNAR

Listhneigðir braskarar innsigla afurðir blankra höfunda
greifynjur mata gjörningalistamenn á demantabruðningi
en hvar eru drykkfelldu heildsalarnir
er héldu uppi oss enn drykkfelldari skáldum
fyrir félagsskap og menningarlegt auðmagn?

horfni heildsali!
ég léti mér nægja
sérsniðin jakkaföt
Þingvallarúntinn
og séniverstár
sem ég velti í munnholinu
meðan ég íhuga mörk listrænna heilinda minna

PASSÉ 3: ROMANTIC POEM
ABOUT CAPITALISTS OF THE PAST

Artistically inclined speculators broker the products of authors
countesses spoon-feed performance artists with diamond dust
but where are the drunk wholesalers
supporting us even more drunk poets
for company and cultural capital?

absent wholesaler!
I would be satisfied
with the custom suit
a drive to Þingvellir
and sips of scotch
that I roll in my mouth
considering the limits of my artistic integrity

OKTÓBERKVÖLD Á LAUGAAFLEGGJARANUM

Það er svo erfitt að ímynda sér fortíðina, reyna að plokka
nútímann út úr myndinni:

trjáræktina rafmagnsstaurana malbikið
sumarbústaðina bílana gámana
brýrnar tjaldstæðið
mig

svo kemur haustmyrkrið
og skyndilega verður allt alveg eins og þá

OCTOBER EVENING ON SECONDARY ROADS

It is so hard to imagine oneself in the past, to try to pluck
the present from the picture:

the planted trees the power lines the pavement
the summer cottages the cars the shipping containers
the bridges the campsite
me

then the autumn dark comes
and suddenly everything is just as it was

EFNI

Við hímum undir skiltinu eins og útigangshross
það syngur í rörum og ískrar í járni
goretexröndin hlykkjast litrík niður hnúkinn
Ísland er land í stöðugri mótun

þeir taka efni við Lambafell
þeir aka efnivið Lambafells
á brott
og setja niður annars staðar

smám saman hverfur Lambafell
en á öðrum stað verður til nýtt land
þar sem áður var sjór og fjara

þegar æðarnar í hjartanu bila
eru teknar æðar úr fótlegg
og settar í staðinn
en vefurinn í fótleggnum grær saman á örskotsstundu

ný fjöll verða til
þar sem þau vantaði áður

við erum land í stöðugri mótun

MATERIAL

we loiter under the sign like wandering horses
the pipes sing and the iron creaks
the colorful goretex-clad line winds down the hill
Iceland is a land in constant formation

they take material from Lambafell
they drive the Lambafell material
away
to set down in another place

gradually Lambafell disappears
but in another place a new land will be made
where before was sea and beach

when blood vessels in the heart fail
veins are taken from the leg
and set in their place
and the leg tissue grows together in no time

new mountains will be
where they were missing before

we are land in constant formation

AUSTURVÖLLUR Á KISTULAGNINGARDAGINN

Föstudagur, sumardagur, sólin skín.
Allir fara úr sokkunum og peysunum og buxunum. Fallegar
stelpur breiða úr teppum á grasinu.
Fallegar stelpur eiga góðan dag, sumardag. Þegar hann er að
kvöldi kominn fara þær út og dansa til morguns og fara heim
með strák eða stelpu og vakna þunnar en hamingjusamar á
nýjum degi, sumardegi.
Það er svimandi ilmur af nýslegnu grasi.
Það eru spriklandi blóm í beðunum.
Höfrungar stökkva á flóanum.
Sólin skín.
Ekkert vantar.
Börn brosa tannlaus í kerrum.
Börn brosa tannlaus í sólina og borða ís sem bráðnar yfir bústnu
hendurnar þeirra. Hnúarnir eru spékoppar í holdinu.
Það er svo hlýtt. Það er engin leið að klæðast svörtu.
Það er engin leið að vera inni í rökkrinu.
Skrifstofumennirnir skella í lás.
Hafið er blátt.
Sólin skín.
Ekkert vantar.
Fólk er komið með ólgandi hreyfingar í mjaðmirnar, fólk langar
að sofa hjá við opnar svaladyr.
Fólk kaupir laxastykki, fólk kaupir lambalundir, fólk ætlar
að grilla í kvöld, brosandi og tjúnað og fá sér í glas.

AUSTURVÖLLUR ON THE DAY OF THE WAKE

Friday, a summer day, the sun is shining.
Everyone sheds socks and sweaters and pants. Beautiful
girls spread blankets on the grass.
Beautiful girls have a good day, a summer day. When night
comes they go out and dance until morning then go home
with a boy or girl and wake up hungover but happy to
a new day, a summer day.
There is a dizzying smell of fresh cut grass.
There are blooms waving in the flower bed.
Dolphins jump in the bay.
The sun is shining.
Nothing is missing.
Children smile toothless in their strollers.
Children smile toothless in the sun and eat ice cream that melts
down their chubby hands. Their knuckles make dimples in their flesh.
It's so warm. There is no way to wear black.
There is no way to stay inside half-lit houses.
Office workers close up shop.
The sea is blue.
The sun is shining.
Nothing is missing.
People start to sway their hips, people want
to make out by open balcony doors.
People buy salmon fillets, people buy lamb steaks, people are going
to grill this evening, smiling and in the mood for a cocktail.

Fólk drekkur bjór og límonaði á kaffihúsunum.
Fallegu stelpurnar hlæja og fallast í faðma.
Rónarnir velta sér fótbrotnir í grasinu.
Gleðin er núna.
Sólin skín og
ekkert vantar.

People drink beer and lemonade in cafes.
Beautiful girls laugh and hug.
Winos roll crippled in the grass.
The joy is now.
The sun is shining and
nothing is missing.

GAMLÁRSKVÖLD

Grá teppi og gráir stólar og
gráir veggir og grá borð og
grá kokteilglös
og grátt faxtæki og grá
dyraumgjörð og gráir nágrannar
og grár stigagangur og grá gata og
grár himinn og bleikir hlaupandi
fætur okkar og nælonskeggið sem við snúum
upp á, hálkan og flugeldarnir
og allt þetta opna lífshættulega rými
okkur til handa

NEW YEAR'S EVE

Gray carpet and gray chairs and
gray walls and gray table and
gray cocktail glasses
and gray fax machine and gray
door frame and gray neighbors
and gray staircase and gray street and
the gray sky and our pale running
feet and the nylon beard we turn
upwards, the slippery ice and fireworks
and all this life-threatening open space
for us

Á HJÚKRUNARDEILDINNI

upplausnin er hér
allt er
á floti
sjálfið
minnið
innbyggði staðsetningarbúnaðurinn
við erum öll hér
en þó annars staðar
og enginn veit hvað gerist næst

IN THE NURSING HOME

the dissolution is here
everything is
afloat
the self
the memory
the built-in locating equipment
we are all here
but also other places
and no one knows what happens next

FALLEGAR RÚSTIR

Skapa það
móta það
ala það
höggva það
skilja það eftir í sólinni gapandi
mót veðri og vindum
sem sverfa það
brjóta það
elska það
forsmá það
taka á sig krók um það
sveipa það dulúð
hluta það niður
og selja
í stykkjum
hjúpa það
og afhjúpa
nota það
marka það
sparka í það
girða það af
rjúfa stífluna
og setja það á kaf
horfa á það
hverfa ofan í jörðina

BEAUTIFUL RUINS

Make it
mold it
birth it
cut it
leave it gaping in the sun
for weather and wind
to grind
break it
love it
scorn it
detour around it
shroud it in mystery
split it
to sell it
in pieces
wrap it up
and unveil it
use it
mark it
kick at it
fence it off
breach the dam
and submerge it
watch it
disappear into the ground

og birtast
úr henni aftur
hefja það
upp fyrir höfuð sér
horfa á það
ljóma

and burst
out of her again
raise it
overhead
watch it
glow

GÓÐIR TÍMAR — útgáfa til upplesturs á leikskólum

Þetta voru kúkatímar. Ég starfaði slitrótt á pissublaðinu, eyddi kvöldunum hamrandi á kúk umvafin prumpufýlu, en á daginn hitti ég gubb. Við sátum á kúkahúsum löngum stundum, oftast á Niðurgangshúsinu þar sem þjónarnir þekktu okkur, drukkum piss og borðuðum kúk. Einhver las línur úr nýjum prumpubálki eða upp úr rassaritgerð, stundum flettum við klósettpappír. Það var mikið pissað, mikið kúkað, svo ráfuðum við um göturnar ölvaðar af eigin píku. Við vorum þarna ég og kúkur, piss, gubb, typpi, prump og fleiri, skítalykt bættist í hópinn ef hún var góð af þeirri viðsjárverðu kúkaþörf sem á það til að fylgja snilligáfunni. Við áttum ekki bót fyrir rassaboruna á okkur en tókst alltaf að skrapa saman fyrir kúk og nýjasta pissi þess ljóðskálds sem við kusum að hæðast að þá stundina. Á endanum prumpuðum við flestar eins og gengur og kúkur heimilislífsins heillaði að vissu leyti — en við héldum auðvitað áfram að pissa meðfram, ævinlega á píkukvöldum, drukkum saman og fórum svo á kúkahús, þar sem við ræddum prump við skörpustu typpi Parísarborgar áður en við fórum með þeim í kúkaherbergið inn af.

GOOD TIMES — version for reading at preschools

Those were poopy times. I worked intermittently on the piss-rag, spending nights hammering a poop, surrounded by a stink cloud, but in the day I met up with barf. We sat at the poop-house for long stretches, often at Diarrheahouse where the servers knew us, drinking pee and eating poo. Someone read lines from a new fart poem or butt essay, sometimes we'd flip through toilet paper. There was a lot of pee, a lot of poop, then we'd stroll through the streets drunk on our own private parts. We were there, poop and I, piss, barf, willy, fart and more, stinker would join the group if she was well enough to risk the need to poop that comes with genius. We didn't have enough for our buttbill but we always managed to scrape something together for the poop and the latest piss by the poet we chose to mock for the moment. In the end we farted like most people and and certainly enjoyed a poopy homelife to some extent—but of course we kept on peeing, every ladybit night, drinking together and then going to the pooper, where we discussed farts with the sharpest willies in Paris before going with them into the pooproom.

PASSÉ 4: VÉR SIGURVEGARAR

svo skoðum við í skúffurnar ykkar
opnum bréfin ykkar
klæðumst fötunum ykkar
lesum dagbækurnar ykkar
túlkum gjörðir ykkar
afhjúpum leyndarmál ykkar

PASSÉ 4: WE THE VICTORS

and so we look in your drawers
we open your letters
wear your clothes
read your diaries
interpret your actions
expose your secrets

ÉG DREG MÖRKIN

Ég dreg mörkin
við ofbeldi

ég dreg mörkin
við eignaspjöll

ég dreg mörkin
við fimm þúsund krónur

ég dreg mörkin
við milljón

ég dreg mörkin
við billjón

ég dreg mörkin
við foreldralaus partí

ég dreg mörkin
við Pólland

ég dreg mörkin
við sjósund

ég dreg mörkin
við þriðja betlarann

I DRAW THE LINE

I draw the line
at violence

I draw the line
at property damage

I draw the line
at five thousand krónur

I draw the line
at a million

I draw the line
at a billion

I draw the line
at unsupervised parties

I draw the line
at Poland

I draw the line
at ocean swimming

I draw the line
at the third hobo

ég dreg mörkin
við slæður

ég dreg mörkin
við geitur

ég dreg mörkin
við bletti í lakinu

ég dreg mörkin
við drenginn með tárið

ég dreg mörkin
við 2004

ég dreg mörkin
við stólpípur

ég dreg mörkin
við sílíkon

ég dreg mörkin
við súran hval

ég dreg mörkin
við dagdrykkju
við reykingar á meðgöngu
við það sem ógnað getur lýðheilsu

I draw the line
at veils

I draw the line
at goats

I draw the line
at stains in the sheets

I draw the line
at the boy in tears

I draw the line
at 2004

I draw the line
at enemas

I draw the line
at silicone

I draw the line
at the acidic whale blubber

I draw the line
at daydrinking
at smoking while pregnant
at that which can threaten public health

ég dreg mörkin
við Kana sem er hérna yfir helgi til að steggja vin sinn

ég dreg mörkin
þar sem mörkin hljóta að liggja

ég dreg mörkin
í hringi og slaufur

ég dreg mörkin

hér eru mörkin

ég dreg mörkin

I draw the line
at the Yank here for his friend's stag weekend

I draw the line
since the line must lie

I draw the line
in rings and bows

I draw the line

here is the line

I draw the line

STORMVIÐVÖRUN

Dagurinn á morgun verður verri
en það þýðir ekki að dagurinn í dag sé ekki slæmur.

Birta Líf Kristinsdóttir
veðurfræðingur

Kaldblár vetur
eilíf nótt á gluggunum
fatahrúgur eru með hæsta móti
perurnar springa ein af annarri
og ég fylgist með myrkrinu leggja undir sig íbúðina

það er kannski djarft að láta sig dreyma um annarra manna vöfflujárn
en það er kalt í Reykjavík og vinir mínir eru ekki hér
ég les minningargreinar um löngu látið fólk
og rækta melankólíuna eins og hjartfólgna plöntu

hvernig getur vetri mögulega átt eftir að ljúka?
hvers vegna að búa um rúmið þegar maður þarf alltaf að sofa í því aftur?
af hverju er svona erfitt að koma í veg fyrir að lýsisflaskan verði
    kámug og sleip?

ég hef líkama minn í taumi eins og stóran björn
sem skilur ekki hvers vegna hann fær ekki að leggjast í híði
sál mína, klyfjahestinn dapureygða, þarf ekki að hafa í taumi;
    eins og ljóðið
lötrar hún þangað sem henni er ætlað

STORMWARNING

The day tomorrow will be worse
but that does not mean that the day today is not bad.

Birta Líf Kristinsdóttir
meteorologist

Coldblue winter
endless night out the windows
the clothing piles are getting high
Light bulbs burst one after another
and I watch the dark take over the apartment

maybe it's bold to let yourself dream about someone else's waffle iron
but it's cold in Reykjavík and my friends aren't here
I read eulogies of people long dead
and tend to my melancholy like a precious plant

how could winter possibly come to an end?
why make the bed when you always need to sleep in it again?
why is it so difficult to keep the fish oil bottle from getting greasy
    and slick?

I have my body by the reins like a big bear
who doesn't understand why he is not lying in a cave
my soul, sad-eyed packhorse, does not need reins;
like the poem she plods where she is expected

þessa dagana er ekkert ferskt
vitundin er súrsuð, þurrkuð og reykt
engar nýjar upplifanir
bara þreyttar minningar

af og til leiftra fyrir augunum
sýnir sem aldrei munu raungerast:
sandur á auðri gangstétt
morgunsól og
ljóstillífunaralsælan í brjóstinu

ég læt ekki glepjast af skynseminni
fleygi strigaskóm og gallajökkum á brennuna

bindið niður trampólínin
bindið niður þakplöturnar
komið grillunum í skjól

these days nothing is fresh
perception is fermented, dried, and smoked
no new experiences
just tired memories

now and then flashes before the eyes
that which will never really happen:
sand on an empty sidewalk
morning sun and
photosynthesizedbliss in the chest

I am not fooled by reason
I throw denim jackets and sneakers on the bonfire

tie down the trampoline
tie down the tarps
get the grills inside

NOTES

"Bubbly in the Vulva"

svo bætti þessi sami fréttamaður gráu ofan á svart

"Add insult to injury" corresponds to the Icelandic expression "put grey on black."

Sportacus is a character from the hit Icelandic but English-speaking TV show *LazyTown*. He is played by gymnastics champion Magnús Scheving, who created the brand to encourage children to live active, healthy lives. Based on Icelandic children's books, a stage adaptation featuring Sportacus as an energetic elf toured Iceland before a TV show was commissioned by Nickelodeon. Produced in American English, the show became an international phenomenon and was dubbed in Icelandic and other languages.

"Retreat to the Waterfall"

"Drekinn" and "Halinn" are geographical references to oceanic areas around Iceland. The Dragon, "Drekinn/Drekasvæðið," is where people are going to search for oil—activities that are being protested by environmental activists. The Tail, "Halinn," is a fishing area near the Westfjords where there have been some terrible storms. In 1925 two fishing trawlers sank and sixty-eight men drowned in a storm that was called Halaveðrið, the Hali weather.

The phrase "and the skull of the deacon gleams white" refers
to the Deacon of Dark River (Djákninn á Myrká), a popular
Icelandic folk tale about a ghost and his betrothed. The deacon
is engaged to a woman named Guðrún. After arranging to
bring her to his farm on Christmas Eve, he is caught in a storm.
He falls into a river, wounds the back of his head on an ice floe,
and drowns. His body is found and buried but word does not
reach Guðrún. His ghost picks her up on Christmas Eve and as
they ride, his hat tips forward and she glimpses the white of his
skull.

"Stormwarning"

For centuries, fermenting, drying, and smoking were the most
common methods of food preservation in Iceland. Today,
Icelanders celebrate their heritage and torment foreign visitors
with delicacies such as acidic whale blubber and sour ram´s
testicles.

A CONVERSATION BETWEEN
AUTHOR AND TRANSLATOR

K.B. Thors: I'm glad we have this opportunity to bring readers into our bunker. We've had a fun dialogue from the get-go, back when I wrote you to ask whether anyone was translating this book. For all our back and forth though, the first time you'd heard my full take on the book as a whole was when *Harvard Review* asked for some poems. The timing was perfect, because I had these, and they asked me to write an introduction to go along with them. We thought it would be a good intro here too, so:

"Slim yet ambitious, *Stormwarning* traces the tension between economic interests and environmental damage with dreadful realism. This matter-of-fact manner also applies to morality and is all the more condemning for Tómasdóttir's calm, self-deprecating delivery. We want to be—or at least to be seen as—good. We are at the mercy of the weather, which has no such concept. Destruction is on the horizon: we hope and fear for it. We continue. We *get the grills inside*. One way or another, we will be satisfied."

Kristín Svava Tómasdóttir: It´s all been such a pleasure! And a pleasant surprise really, that the whole book would end up being translated and published abroad. That´s not very common and not necessarily something I would have expected. I remember being so happy about your description of the book in the *Harvard Review*. It's always good to have the feeling that someone gets what you're doing.

The whole prospect of the poems being read by non-Icelanders, in another language and another cultural context, is just very exciting. I recently listened to an American podcast series where a recent translation of one of my favourite Icelandic novels, *Tómas Jónsson, Bestseller* by Guðbergur Bergsson, was being studied, and it was so inspiring to hear literary enthusiasts discuss the book from a totally fresh angle, unaffected by old local politics and prejudices. I love translation in general—it's part of a common sharing of literature and literary interaction that is so important, and vital for a small community like Iceland.

KBT: Speaking of cultural context, let's dive into the poems! There was a funny moment when I sent the first draft of these translations to my aunt, gracious answerer of my Icelandic questions. Re: vúlvunni (the vulva) she said something like "hmm... maybe that is the name of a club?". I thought it was a rhetorical vulva—a cheeky celebration, and recipe for a yeast infection. Then it turned out to be an actual place! If not a drinking hole per se, then a co-op?

KST: Well, yes — it originally derives from me and my friends' nickname for our office facility. I belong to a gang of literary-minded women that was formed around a book blog many years ago. Some of us share an office that we call, with ironic affection, the Vulva. So from a personal standpoint, it's a wink to a small community that has given me invaluable artistic support through the years, as well as a lot of practical advice—for example on tax returns. But it is also a celebration of female company, bubbly, and decadence in general.

I like putting private jokes into my poetry—they're fun because they're often so random and absurd, and I like absurdities — but I never do it unless I feel it works without the background knowledge. I dislike namedropping in literature. Of course you're always writing in some cultural context, but if the references are too heavy-handed, they easily become exclusive and I want books to work on the most basic level too. I still haven't forgiven the Spanish academic I read an interview with once who claimed you couldn't really appreciate Jaime Gil de Biedma's poetry without having read the Greeks. I guess he thought he was elevating Gil de Biedma—whose poetry I love, even if I've read very little of the Greeks—but I thought he was being quite condescending both to him and his readers. Give them some bubbly in the Vulva, I say!

KBT: Free pours all round! I like when there are layers to a work, when poems build on what came before, but we're all coming from our own reading and life soup anyway. Maybe it's the way allusions are handled. A couple years ago it seemed like Hegel and Kant were getting sprinkled all over the place—but they alone don't make a poem or drag it to some higher brow. Anne Carson incorporates them, but she makes them feel like characters in conversation. You manage a similar effect with details rather than names. Parking illegally in Sweden in "Do not," the series of larger stops in "I draw the line" that make the reader imagine what you're referring to—things like Poland, 2004, enemas...

KST: "Do not" and "I draw the line" are sister poems. The form is similar and they deal with the same theme: The difference between what we are, what we say and what we do—how people narrate their own self and life, what is emphasized and what not, and what that says about the things that society wants us to be and do.

A few years ago I read a book that I was unexpectedly very influenced by: *Rubbish! The Archaeology of Garbage*. It´s about researchers of contemporary archaeology who dive into landfills and people´s trash bins, going through scraps, wrappers, diapers, bottles and cans, porn magazines, and all sorts of garbage juices, and derive from them conclusions about consumption, waste, class division. In some instances they made people fill out questionnaires about their own consumption and of course people wildly exaggerated the amount of vegetables that they ate but diminished the amount of red meat and sugar—even if they *knew* that the researchers were going through their trash.

This I find fascinating. It´s not that we´re telling intentional lies, we´re just constructing this narrative about ourselves, in a way that makes it a bit easier to be us. Giving certain words and actions meaning. Telling ourselves and others what we would never do, for example, because that´s just not who we are, because we are good. When writing the two poems I used those familiar phrases and mixed them together with material that I wrote, stuff that I overheard somewhere and stuff I found on the internet—which accounts for some of the weirder lines!

KBT: "Do not" and "Another letter to Mr. Brown" put the speaker in the hot seat. That's so much more effective than accusing others of hypocrisy. I wonder how many readers are relieved to read about someone else's morally iffy behaviour.

Your dad, Tómas R. Einarsson, is an accomplished musician. "I draw the line" and "Do Not" wound up as lyrics on one of his many jazz albums, *Bongó*, and you were nominated for an Icelandic Music Award for best lyrics! How has music influenced your writing style? Your use of repetition in line and steady phrasing acts as a kind of backbone, rhythmic and more ominous as the book goes on.

KST: I like repetition as a flexible way to create rhythm and structure, and I do like both my music and my poetry to have strong rhythm. This may be related to the fact that readings have always been my favorite part of poetry. For me that´s the "original" version of my poems, when I read them out loud to an audience, even if I also put them on paper and collect them in books.

It´s interesting that you pair "Another letter to Mr. Brown" with "Do not" and "I draw the line." Maybe it could be considered a precursor to those poems. It is one of four poems in this book that were not in the Icelandic original of *Stormwarning* from 2015. "Another letter to Mr. Brown" and "Good times" are from

83

my previous book, *Skrælingjasýningin* or *The Savages Exhibition*, which was published in Iceland in 2011, the alternative version of "Good times" was published in a literary magazine around the same time, and "Beautiful ruins" I wrote more recently for a specific project.

"Another letter to Mr. Brown" is rooted in a certain political situation: Mr. Brown is British prime minister Gordon Brown and the poem is written post-crash, when British anti-terrorism laws were used to recoup money that Brits had in the failed Icelandic banks. It is inspired by some Icelanders´ response to the British move—which was to be very offended that anyone would think that *we* could be guilty of terrorism.

The title of the book, *The Savages Exhibition*, refers to a colonial exhibition organized by the Danish in Copenhagen in 1905, where they exhibited people and objects from their colonies in the Caribbean and the North Atlantic. Icelandic students in Copenhagen protested angrily—not because they had anything against the exhibition per se, but because they were offended by the idea that they themselves would be put on display with people that they considered to be savages. The poem could be seen as a comment on Icelandic nationalism, but also on a complex situation where Icelanders constantly try to to prove that they are a part of what is considered to be "the civilized world"—white, Western, etc.—but are often exoticized themselves.

The poem is obviously quite chaotic and not as regular as "Do not" and "I draw the line," but it has that mix I like of everyday language and stranger and more stylized lines. When we were discussing "Another letter to Mr. Brown," you said that the narrator felt prim, and I agree with that — but with a few glasses of red in her. "Prim but drunk" is my new favorite narrative voice.

I'm particularly happy that we could add "Good times" to this book. It's one of my favorite poems from my 2011 book and even if the style is on the distant and ironic side, the poem feels personal, almost manifesto-like. Since I was a teenager, I have been very conscious of how ever-present the ideal of the male genius is in the literary world and how it seems to inspire a curious mix of inferiority complex and megalomania in boys with artistic dreams. It is of course usually accompanied by some kind of rejection of the physical and the female, which tends to stand in the way of the guys reaching the sublime. I wrote "Good times" after I read Luis Buñuel's autobiography, which has a constant flood of male bigshots—plus two women sidekicks who come across as absolutely obnoxious and disruptive of intellectual and emotional male growth.

Included here is also an alternative version of "Good times," meant for preschoolers, which may require some explanation. Many years ago, a few other poets drove to a village not far from Reykjavík, where we participated in a small art festival. We were supposed to read in locations like the primary school, the fish factory, the gas station, and then ended up reading for a group of young school kids at the village's sport center. They of course didn't understand a thing of our scathing political criticism and lyrical innovations, they were incredibly bored and it was all rather unfortunate. The one time the children showed any emotion was when one of the poems mentioned toilet paper.

After that experience I decided to come prepared if I ever read to small children again—I would come stacked with their favorite references to defecation and genitalia. For a while I only read the poem to adults, which was good practice in tackling my own bourgeois sense of shame, in front of painfully silent audiences. Later I had a chance to actually read it to a large group of children—and felt like a rock star. There were encores and autographs. It was great.

KBT: "Another letter to Mr. Brown" and both "Good times" definitely fit with the other poems, though they weren't in the original Icelandic version of *Stormwarning*. "Passé 3" and "~" come to mind. It's neat to see a writer's timeline run through their books, and including them feels like it lets English readers further into your world.

I'm a huge fan of the preschool version of "Good times"! It was the last poem you sent to me as a maybe for this book, not sure what our editors would think, but the good folks at Phoneme didn't bat an eye. To me the versions are a dual manifesto, first roasting that gendered genius and then our general human pretense that we transcend poop. It reminds me of when we read in Reykjavík and as I was making notes of the multi-lingual graffiti in the all-gendered bathrooms, you suggested we make poems out of them and close out the night reading those! The audience seemed to enjoy it—your tackling of that bourgeois shame releases some of its hold on others.

On the translation level, I'm particularly happy to be able to address "lady bits," the lack of language for women's bodies. Willy, pecker, johnson, there are lots of kid-friendly terms for penis. We're short on feminine correspondents, at least in my experience. Whether we're talking about vaginas or vulvas is another issue—people often say vagina when they mean vulva, which is part of why your first page is such a joy. In Icelandic the alternate "Good times" uses "pussy," which is way too strong in English, so I went looking for girl-part words. Apparently Mary and foof are go-tos for some parents. Foof! Nothing felt vernacular to the extent that it wouldn't stick out of the poem like a sore thumb. "Private parts" is common, but not gender specific.

To me, the original "Good times" high-fives "Bubbly in the Vulva," poking at those old boys clubs and the reality that those scenes and great works come from people just hanging out. That in itself is a luxury, but not necessarily shrouded in mystique.

I can't imagine what it's like to move through the world in that male default, not only unfettered but with pervasive encouragement. It was satisfying to find Simone, and the speaker, and that group of women—Svava included—not only at the center of the café but also getting married, rather than being creative spinsters, and going to the whorehouse. Why wouldn't they?

I'm curious about the role of honesty in swiveling around ideas of access and the sublime. In "Stormwarning," melancholy is actively tended, the body by the reins highlights the person behind those outward actions. Self-awareness, confession, and a waffle iron, which threw me for a loop on first read.

KST: I might have been stretching it a bit with the waffle iron! It's one of those random things that found their way from my surroundings into poetry. There it became a part of the bigger melancholy of the poem—a distant promise of waffle making and warmth. I wrote most of *Stormwarning* during the winter of 2014-2015, which was a stormy one. "The day tomorrow will be worse, but that does not mean that the day today is not bad" is an actual quote from meteorologist Birta Líf Kristinsdóttir. She said it in March 2015, when we had three separate storm warnings on the same weekend. (Her name adds to the irony: "Birta" means *light*, "Líf" means *life*.)

Many people naturally assume that Iceland must be cold, but the tricky thing about living here is rather that the weather is very volatile—we just have a lot of *bad weather*. The country's geographical position also means that the winters are dark. You go to work in the morning in the dark and it's dark again when you go home, and it's always raining and snowing and raining and hailing and freezing and thawing and freezing again. Tying down trampolines really is a regular act for many an Icelander. Then when spring comes there's suddenly all this overwhelming light and energy. It's very unstable.

I'm quite fascinated by how intricately these natural fluctuations are connected with one's body and state of mind. It's a very feminist issue, of course, the inseparability of body and spirit, and links back to what I said earlier about the idea of the male genius as something untouched by physical limitations. I have the same dislike for any romanticized version of physical or natural (or female) purity. We're all one big mess. And it's the mess that I want, the mixing of the natural and the man-made, the guts and the brains.

KBT: That line from Birta Líf Kristinsdóttir makes me laugh every time, especially in the context of a meteorologist talking to the public. It's to the point, optimistic, and scary—it could always be worse.

Your interest in nature and our states of body and mind comes through in so many ways, and with remarkable warmth and humor. "My Flu" is a keen blend of the physical and psychological that lays further ground for "Stormwarning." I think this project came together so well partly because I'm mostly interested in the same mess—how natural elements shape humanity, how we forget and remember we are animals.

KST: I´m glad to hear that. I think I have quite an ironic sense of humor, but I find irony tiring if it´s too monotonous. Again, it´s the nuances and ambiguities that interest me most, both thematically and linguistically.

How do you think that a non-Icelandic audience will experience these poems? What do you think that they will find familiar and what not?

KBT: I'm curious about that too! I think there will be a range, of course. Self-conceptions and social politics are everywhere, though I imagine your frank approach will be refreshing for many readers. Here we are again—I don't want you to be pigeonholed as characteristically Icelandic, though you must be, somehow.

I tried to explain in the translator's note that part of why these poems resonate with such power, for me, is because of a shared environment, family culture, etc. I may be too close to answer this question well, but I think there are thrills in the new as well as the recognizable.

"New Year's Eve" comes to mind. Many people don't have the visceral experience of "life-threatening open space" that the poem mentions, though I think the entitlement at the end is a universal nerve. When I go home to Alberta—Big Sky Country— after being in a city, I am always struck and relieved by the space. Driving for hours without seeing many signs of humanity does chill the stomach though, as you realize how vulnerable we are. It's a terrible reality, not positive or negative terror but desolate and sublime. That poem hits home for someone with that experience, but also offers it to readers who may not have been in that position. "Being positive" and "Material" are similar in that way, I think. Readers who may not be able to relate are brought in so that they can share that perspective.

Remember when, as the book was coming together, I emailed you about the "sand on an empty sidewalk" in "Stormwarning"? We were combing through, catching Canadian "ou"s, and I realized that a California reader would probably take that image much differently than we do! To me it's the sand left after the snow melts, remnants of trying to get traction and safety. I thought about clarifying that, but it would have cluttered the poem and crossed the line into pandering. How many nuggets like that are embedded in these lines? That's why I asked if there was hidden meaning in the waffle iron!

KST: Oh, the thought of sneakers and sand on a sidewalk! For a sun-starved Icelander in the middle of the winter, it has an almost visceral effect.

KBT: Even if people don't feel that sand sidewalk in their guts, it has psychological power. The final arrival of spring, a thaw, or the wind blowing the beach into the city—they're all nature layered over human paths. My favorite aspect of "Stormwarning" and *Stormwarning* is the conduit they create between environmental crisis and internal malaise.

Hopefully, as with every translation, the familiar and foreign are reason to read further, and the ground shifts with every read. I hope this book also compels readers to keep an ear out for younger voices—especially vulvic punks, in the widest sense— and everyone out there tending liminal bonfires. We'll have to see. Stock up on corkscrews and batten down the hatches.

TRANSLATOR'S NOTE

Icelandic literature is often associated with myths, sagas, and pop culture adaptations. With a language spoken by relatively few people, translation attention falls on the literary giants, of which Iceland has a hefty share.

I began translating as a way to spice up my Icelandic studies. It was a fun break from grammar exercises and lessons, but I was generally reading established, canonical stuff. I wanted to know what was happening on the ground, being written by writers less likely to be in the spotlight. I was lucky enough to have recently interviewed Sjón for *Asymptote*, so I wrote him to ask if he could recommend exciting contemporary Icelandic writers. I was particularly curious about women, in the broadest sense, no pun intended, and non-binary writers, knowing as we do the statistics on publishing, translation, and gender. He responded with a short list of names and emails, Kristín Svava's among them. *Stormwarning* had just come out in Iceland. The title struck a chord, I wrote to her, and soon the book arrived in the mail. The moment I opened it to "Bubbly in the Vulva" was one of kismet fizz.

Icelandic culture is paradoxical. Intense locality mixes with an awareness of global forces, if not out of interest then out of necessity—smaller animals have to keep an eye out. Resource and tourist economies are at odds with the island's environment and Kristín's work articulates those conflicts in sharp, post-crash stride. On a social level, allusions are more direct in a country with such a tight-knit population. People are more familiar with scandals and business deals when there are fewer degrees of separation. The interest this creates is amplified by Kristín's background as a historian—her poetic presentation of facts is underpinned by expertise in the country's political and natural landscape.

In the summer of 2017 I had a residency with the Writer's Union of Iceland, where Kristín happened to be working. We did a summer solstice ljóðakvöld—poetry evening—in a bar in Reykjavík, and watching her read again days later gave me a better sense of the solidity of her stage presence. Then we road tripped to Snæfellsnes, driving some of the routes from "October Evening on Secondary Roads" on a pilgrimage to the water library at Stykkishólmur.

It was a joy to work so directly with a poet whose ear and sensibility is strong even in English. Kristín's experience as a translator contributed to this book in ways I cannot define. I find a satisfying bulk in Icelandic's ability to denote meaning in few, perhaps long, words. Though English spaces things out, I believe I've maintained the rhythm and mood of Kristín's originals. Her tone is deceptively casual and conveying that was a priority in this work.

A sense of humor is vital to these poems. They take scenes and subcultures to task in few words; the darker the subject, the more funny potential. A strange gift of this project for me was realizing that I admire Kristín's comedic ability in much the same way I do my dad's, and my Icelandic uncle Marinó's. Growing up with that concise sarcasm helped immensely as I tried to get at the deadpan nature of these poems.

Embedded in those dark laughs is an intimacy with weather, and winter in particular. My experience with deep cold, dark days, and rural areas that question the passage of time are part of why this work resonates with me and why I am so happy to see it reaching English readers, perhaps especially those in different climates. These poems are an interplay of inheritance, personality, similarity, and difference, and I hope this book, Phoneme's catalogue, and translation in general inspire readers to study outside their native tongues and engage the formative power of the words we use.

Phoneme's decision to produce bilingual editions of this and other books is a boon for language learners and nerds. I hope that readers enjoy the visuals of the Icelandic text, the otherness of the alphabet, the English words I compound to get at the Icelandic originals, and all of these reminders that language is something we build.

This project has taught me a great deal about creative community. I'm thankful to Sjón for his generosity, Kit Schluter for his advice, and spaces like Wendy's Subway in Bushwick, where the first conversation about publishing this book in English took place. I'm grateful to David Shook for his work publishing diverse world literature, as well as Hannah Jakobsen, who was wonderful to work with, the Phoneme team, and all the translators out there. Extra special thanks to Ellen Nína Ingolfsson for her enthusiastic lessons, and to Thor, for everything.

ACKNOWLEDGMENTS

Thank you to the *Scandinavian Review, Harvard Review,* and *EuropeNow,* where selections of these translations previously appeared.

BIOGRAPHIES

Kristín Svava Tómasdóttir (b.1985) has been active on the Icelandic poetry scene since her teenage years. Her poems have been translated into English, Danish, German, Finnish, Polish, Portuguese, Italian, Spanish and Arabic. Her own translations of Valerie Solanas´s feminist manifesto *SCUM* and Cuban author Virgilio Piñera´s poem *La isla en peso* have been published in Icelandic. Tómasdóttir holds an MA degree in History from the University of Iceland. Her most recent work is a book on the history of pornography in Iceland.

K.B. Thors is a poet and translator whose poems have appeared in publications across the U.S., U.K., and Canada. Her debut poetry collection *Vulgar Mechanics* is forthcoming from Coach House Books in 2019. An Icelandic-Ukrainian Canadian from rural Alberta, Canada, Thors's translations from Icelandic and Spanish have appeared in *The Harvard Review, The Scandinavian Review, Circumference,* and *Palabras Errantes.* Her translation of *Chintungo: The Story of Someone Else* by Soledad Marambio is available from Ugly Duckling Presse. She holds a BA in Philosophy from the University of Alberta and an MFA in Creative Writing from Columbia University, where she became a Teaching Fellow in Poetry. She is also a performance artist and educator who before teaching writing worked in a sex-positive, woman-positive, and body-positive sex shop.

CPSIA information can be obtained
at www.ICGtesting.com
Printed in the USA
LVOW12s1942130418
573405LV00001B/1/P